Trafalgar 200
International Fleet Review
A Pictorial Record

Previous page - The larger ships of the Fleet Review at anchor in the Eastern anchorage. The French aircraft carrier FS Charles de Gaulle sits behind the bows of the American Assault Ship USS Saipan. HM Ships Bulwark and Ocean can be seen in the background. (Maritime Photographic)

Published by Maritime Books, Lodge Hill, Liskeard, Cornwall PL14 4EL, England

Printed and bound in Malta by Gutenberg Press.

Author's Notes

Having the good fortune to find myself in Portsmouth for the Trafalgar 200 International Fleet Review I was able to witness first hand the magnificent gathering of warships, tall ships and merchantmen from around the world. Stretched along the Solent for an incredible 7 miles I was struck by the fact that it was such a fleeting event that there was perhaps a need to have a longer lasting record. However, as the week passed the thought was put to the back of my mind. Until, that is, I returned to the office, following the International Festival of the Sea, to find a mountain of messages all asking the same thing - "Are you going to do a book?"
Fortunately, there was an equally large pile of CDs with hundreds of images taken from a myriad of both professional and amateur photographers. It would appear that with the advent of the digital camera there is no limit to how many pictures a photographer is willing to take!
This then is the result of many hours sifting through hundreds of images and gradually filtering them down to a manageable number in order to produce a worthy photographic record of the event.
I have been able to include at least one picture of every warship present, together with a selection of those tall ships and merchantmen for which we had images. If your particular vessel does not appear, it is for no other reason than we didn't have a picture submitted - some ships it would appear are more photogenic than others.
This book is intended, not as a literary historical record, more a photographic album of images to record the events and the participants. In the hope that a picture really does paint a thousand words, this collection of images should speak volumes.

A Japanese Training Squadron rides at anchor with other international warships and merchant ships during the Fleet Review rehearsal day. (Crown Copyright/Ministry of Defence)

THE WHITE ENSIGN ASSOCIATION LIMITED

A REGISTERED CHARITY. LIMITED BY GUARANTEE, CHARITY No. 206787

HMS BELFAST
TOOLEY STREET
LONDON SE1 2JH
Telephone 020 7407 8658
MOD: 9621 81945
FAX: 020 7357 6298
EMail:office@whiteensign.co.uk
Web: www.whiteensign.co.uk

Admiral Sir Jock Slater GCB LVO DL
Chairman

The White Ensign Association is delighted to be associated with this pictorial record of the Trafalgar 200 International Fleet Review in the Solent. Our Council and staff were all present on an historic and splendid day and many were embarked in MY LEANDER, owned by our President, Commodore Sir Donald Gosling Kt KCVO RNR; she can be seen on the superb cover photograph of this book.

The White Ensign Association has been a source of guidance and advice for serving and retired members of the naval service and their families since 1958. Acting rather like a "citizens advice bureau" for naval people, the Association focuses on financial guidance and employment advice and also covers most areas of personal administration. With the specialist help of its supporters, the Association assists some 4000 people every year. The service is impartial and absolutely free. To find out more about our work, visit our web site at **www.whiteensign.co.uk**.

The belief that seafarers are very special people motivates the work of our staff at the Association. The 28th July 2005, in the 200th year after the Battle of Trafalgar, was a very special day in the nation's maritime history. This record will serve as a marvellous reminder of a magnificent occasion for those who were present and a vivid illustration of the day for those not so fortunate.

Jock Slater

August 2005

Introduction

A gathering of warships is always a memorable event - a large Fleet Review even more so. There have been many such gatherings in the Solent over the centuries celebrating hard won battles, commemorating Coronations, Jubilees or even assembling before the monarch prior to setting sail to meet the enemy - whatever the reason for the gathering, such a concentration of military might has never failed to impress.

For me, this was my second Fleet Review. In 1977 I was a mere schoolboy, with a fascination for the Royal Navy. I knew that I had to see the assembled fleet, and so set off from Coventry with a schoolfriend - destination Portsmouth. I remember little of the journey. It was I am sure on a coach, but was I bunking off from school? Had I got permission? To tell the truth I can't recall. What I do remember is standing on Southsea sea front among a crowd of thousands, peering out into the Solent to grab a glimpse of a warship amongst the low cloud and drizzle which seemed determined to spoil my day. I got no further than the seafront - I just stood there in awe of the numerous grey hulls which appeared at irregular intervals through the squalls and then just as quickly were swallowed up again - but the memory remains, just as vivid today as it was in 1977 (and I don't even recall how, or when, I got back to Coventry!)

It was with some trepidation that I heard of plans for the Trafalgar 200 International Fleet Review. The Royal Navy had shrunk so much in the intervening years. Could it really be a spectacle with so few warships to choose from? As it turned out there was no need to worry. The organisers had sent invitations around the world and navies from far and wide had taken up the opportunity and headed to the Solent to commemorate what was possibly one of the most defining events, not only in the history of naval warfare, but also in defining the future course and shape of world history.

There have been many large reviews at Spithead, the first as far back as 1415 when King Henry V reviewed his ships before going to do battle with the French.

Queen Victoria was very keen on Fleet Reviews, witnessing no less than 17 during her reign, though the 1897 Diamond Jubilee Review and the 1899 Review were presided over by the Prince of Wales, due to the monarch's frailty.

Fleet Reviews also witnessed revolutionary changes in the shape of naval warfare. The review of 1856 witnessed the first of the ironclad ships, the beginning of the end of the traditional wooden hulled fighting ship. By 1867 at a review held for the Sultan of Turkey HMS Warrior and HMS Black Prince were in attendance, together with the powerful five masted HMS Minotaur. Of note this was also the first Fleet Review where every Royal Navy ship flew the White Ensign, the old Red, White and Blue Squadrons being no more.

The largest review ever held at Spithead was, remarkably, never advertised. Held in May 1944, 800 vessels of the D-Day Invasion fleet were reviewed. Subsequent reviews have seen the rise of the aircraft carrier (1935 and 1937), the last of the battleships (1953) and the first appearance of nuclear powered warships (1977).

Billed as the largest ever gathering of international warships the world has ever seen, the Trafalgar 200 International Fleet Review took place on 28 June 2005.

Although the previous days had been very hot and clear, the weather forecasters warned of a fast moving weather front coming up the channel and had predicted a day of thunderstorms and torrential rain. It was with a great sense of relief that I opened my hotel room curtains on the morning of the 28th to find the weather clear and sunny.

Over 150 ships had gathered and rehearsed the days events. At the appointed time the review column set out from Portsmouth and headed for the Solent. Led by the Trinity House Vessel Patricia, HMS Endurance, acting as the Royal Yacht followed, with HMS Chatham, HMS Scott, HMS Enterprise, RFA Sir Bedivere, MY Leander and the tall ship Grand Turk completing the reviewing ships.

As the review progressed, it seemed that the weather predictions were gaining credibility. As the Royal Yacht headed west through the assembled ships, the skies began to darken and the wind to freshen. By the time HMS Endurance had anchored at the head of the assembled fleet for the steampast and air display, the weather had closed in and the heavens had opened - but with true British spirit the thousands of spectators remained glued to their viewing spot, not wishing to give up their place and risk missing any of the remaining spectacle - in fact with the rain lashing on their heads and the sea lapping at their feet, many went the whole hog and decided that a swim was the order of the day!

Undeterred by the atrocious weather the flying display continued and with the arrival of the Red Arrows at 1730 the weather was beginning to break.

By the time of the big finale, a "Son et Lumiere" show recreating a Nelsonian battle, the weather was once again dry. The battle re-enactment had been surrounded by controversy as it was announced before the event that the battle was not a recreation of the Battle of Trafalgar, more a depiction of a Nelsonian era battle and, in order to save any blushes amongst visiting crews, the two sides would be red and blue! Fortunately no-one had told the narrator of the event and the sound and light spectacular was accompanied by rousing narrative of the British rout of the combined French and Spanish Fleets!

A spectacular firework display brought to an end an event unlikely to be repeated for a generation.

Had it lived up to its billing as a once in a lifetime, not to be missed, naval spectacular?

You bet it did!

Steve Bush
August 2005

International Fleet Review 2005 - Participants

ROYAL NAVY, ROYAL FLEET AUXILIARY & ARMY

Aircraft Carriers (CVS)

R05	HMS Invincible	Cdre N Morisetti (Local Capt in Command)
R06	HMS Illustrious	Cdre R G Cooling (Local Capt in Command)

Amphibious Assault Ships (LPH/LPD)

L12	HMS Ocean	Cdre C A Johnstone-Burt (Local Capt in Command)
L14	HMS Albion	Capt K Winstanley
L15	HMS Bulwark	Capt J H Stanford

Antarctic Patrol Ship

A171	HMS Endurance	Capt T M Karsten

Type 22 Frigates

F87	HMS Chatham	Capt S J Chick
F85	HMS Cumberland	Capt R R Best

Nuclear-powered Submarines (SSN)

	Trenchant	Cdr H D Beard
	Turbulent	Cdr A L Coles
	Trafalgar	Cdr M H Williams

Type 42 Destroyers

D108	Cardiff	Cdr M J D Beardall
D89	Exeter	Cdr A W Reed OBE
D96	Gloucester	Cdr R M Tuppen
D91	Nottingham	Cdr S Holt
D90	Southampton	Cdr R C Vitali

Type 23 Frigates

F80	Grafton	Cdr R J A Bellfield
F234	Iron Duke	Cdr A A Jordan
F229	Lancaster	Cdr J D Morley
F233	Marlborough	Cdr I E Graham
F236	Montrose	Cdr A J Webb
F83	St Albans	Cdr S Dainton
F237	Westminster	Cdr A Betton

Survey Ships

H88	Enterprise	Cdr V A Nail
H131	Scott	Cdr S R Malcom
H130	Roebuck	Lt Cdr J E Churcher
H86	Gleaner	Lt S Weaver

Fishery Protection Vessel

P281	Tyne	Lt Cdr J M Lowther

Mine Counter Measure Vessels (MCM)

M31	Cattistock	Lt Cdr J R Barnes
M37	Chiddingfold	Lt Cdr K M T Houlberg
M34	Middleton	Lt Cdr P L Allen
M30	Ledbury	Lt Cdr R Wilson
M109	Bangor	Lt Cdr D R Wilson
M108	Grimsby	Lt Cdr N P May
M107	Pembroke	Lt Cdr S J Ryan
M110	Ramsey	Lt Cdr M C Mackey
M104	Walney	Lt Cdr J E Beadsmoore

MCM on Sentinel Duty

M112	Shoreham	Lt Cdr I F Lower
M106	Penzance	Lt Cdr B Ripley

P2000 Training Craft

P264	Archer	Lt S L Scott
P270	Blazer	Lt A E Pollard
P165	Example	Lt C J Wyness
P164	Explorer	Lt A C Mason
P291	Puncher	Lt T J Berry
P275	Raider	Lt G R Palin
P293	Ranger	Lt J M B Parkin
P274	Tracker	Lt P A Kohn
P294	Trumpeter	Lt A Smith

Royal Fleet Auxiliaries

A135	Argus	Capt S H Cant
A388	Fort George	Capt J Murchie
A387	Fort Victoria	Capt W M Walworth OBE
A110	Orangeleaf	Capt T Iles
L3005	Sir Galahad	Capt F Brady
L3505	Sir Tristram	Capt P M Farmer
L3004	Sir Bedivere	Capt M Jarvis
A390	Wave Ruler	Capt D Worthington
	MV Hurst Point	Capt B Kay
L110	Aachen	WO2 Houghton
L111	Arezzo	SSgt Holland
L113	Audemer	SSgt Golby

RN UNITS ON SECURITY PATROL

Type 42 Destroyer

D95	*Manchester*	*Cdr W Q F Evans*

Type 23 Frigate

F235	*Monmouth*	*Cdr J P Kyd*
F81	*Sutherland*	*Cdr P J Haslam*

Castle Class Offshore Patrol Vessel

P258	*Leeds Castle*	*Lt Cdr C D Goodsell*

Hunt Class Patrol Vessels

M29	*Brecon*	*Lt Cdr C P Atkinson*
M32	*Cottesmore*	*Lt D S Knight*
M35	*Dulverton*	*Lt L R Hayashi*

FOREIGN & COMMONWEALTH NAVAL VESSELS

Algerian Navy

353	*El Kirch*	*Cmdt L Bouhacene*
Senior Officer Embarked		*Lt Col A Tabali*

Australian Navy

150	*HMAS Anzac*	*Capt R T Menhinick*
Flag Officer Embarked		*VAdm C Ritchie*

Canadian Navy

336	*HMCS Montreal*	*Cdr P Dempsey*

Belgian Navy

F911	*BNS Westdiep*	*Cdr SG C Rijckaert*
A960	*BNS Godetia*	*Cdr JG J Lucaretti*
M923	*BNS Narcis*	*Lt Cdr Terasson*

Brazilian Navy

U20	*NE Cisne Branco*	*Capt P V C Rodrigues Jr*

Colombian Navy

BE160	*ARC Gloria*	*Capt J Morales*

Danish Navy

L17	*HDMS Esbern Snare*	*Cdr S G S Meyer*

Estonian Navy

A230	*Admiral Pitka*	*Lt(SG) U Saska*

Finnish Navy

01	*SMS Pohjanmaa*	*Lt Cdr S Laine*
Senior Officer Embarked		*Capt(N) K Varsio*

French Navy

R91	*FS Charles de Gaulle*	*Capt X Magne*
Flag Officer Embarked		*VAdm J Mazar*
D615	*FS Jean Bart*	*Capt P Ausser*
A607	*FS Meuse*	*Cdr A Camus*
S606	*FS Perle*	*Cdr Martin*
A650	*FS La Belle Poule*	*Lt L Chapuis*
A652	*FS Mutin*	*CPO S Sxay*
A676	*FS Saire*	

German Navy

F219	*FGS Sachsen*	*FrgKpt V Buller*
Senior Officer Embarked		*FrgKpt M Dirks*
M1066	*FGS Frankenthal*	*Lt Cdr K Altfuldisch*
	FGS Asta	*Cdr S G Schoeneborn*

Greek Navy

F452	*HS Hydra*	*Cdr I Pattas*

Indian Navy

D62	*INS Mumbai*	*Capt S Lanba*
	TS Tarangini	*Cdr M Asthana*

Indonesian Navy

	KRI Dewa Ruci	*Lt Col Sutarrnono*

Irish Navy

P31	*LE Eithne*	*Cdr M Mellet*

Italian Navy

A5312	*ITS Amerigo Vespucci*	*Capt V M Billardello*
S523	*ITS Giuliano Prini*	*Lt Cdr L Del Monaco*

Japanese Navy

3508	*JDS Kashima*	*Capt K Mukai*
Flag Officer Embarked		*RAdm M Shibata*
101	*JDS Murasame*	*Cdr K Chizo*
153	*JDS Yuugiri*	*Cdr M Fujiwara*

Latvian Navy

A53	*LNS Virsatis*	*LSG U Zupa*

Lithuanian Navy

M51	*LNS Kursis*	*Lt(N) G Premeneckas*

Moroccan Navy

611	*Mohammed V*	*Capt M Tahin*

Nertherlands Navy

L800	*HrMs Rotterdam*	*Capt P J Bindt*

M861 HrMs Urk — Lt Cdr Fievez
Y8050 TS Urania — Lt Cdr P C B Dijkhuizen

Nigeria
F89 NNS Aradu — Cdre B A Raji

Oman Navy
Q32 RNOV Al Mua'zzar — Cdr A Bin Saif Bin Abdullah Al Sadairi
S-1 RNOV Shabab Oman — Cdr C Biggins

Pakistani Navy
185 PNS Tippu Sultan — Capt I Saeed
20 PNS Moawin — Capt M Ahmed
Flag Officer Embarked — Cdre A Sandila

Polish Navy
273 ORP General Tadeus Kosciuszko — Cdr M Polinski
253 ORP Iskra — Lt Cdr R Zywiec

Portuguese Navy
A520 NRP Sagres — Capt A C V R Carrilho
F331 NRP Alvares Cabral — Cdr L C de Sousa Pereira

Romanian Navy
222 RS Regina Maria — Cdr V Borsaru

Russian Navy
605 RFS Admiral Levchenko — Capt 2R A P Dolgov
Senior Officer Embarked — Capt 1R A Shuvanov
Flag Officer Embarked — Adm M Abramov

Serbian Navy
SMAF Jadran — Cdr M Katic

South African Navy
A301 SAS Drakensburg — Capt C R Sharwood

South Korean Navy
975 ROKS Chungmugong Yi Sun-Shin — Capt Chung- Kee Park
57 ROKS Chun Jee — Capt Jin Su Lee
Flag Officer Embarked — RAdm Yum-Hee Choi

Spanish Navy
R11 SPS Principe de Asturias — Capt J M G-Bouza Marzo
Flag Officer Embarked — RAdm J Palomino Ulla
F103 SPS Blas de Lezo — Cdr M de la Puente Mora-Figuera

Turkish Navy
F245 TCG Orucries — Cdr E Kucukerol

Uruguayan Navy
20 ORU Capitain Miranda — Capt R Anon

United States Navy
2 USS Saipan — Capt Donna Looney

United States Coastguard
USCG Eagle — Capt E J Shaw

TALL SHIPS

Bulgaria
TS Kaliakra — Capt I Lazarov

France
Schooner La Recouvrance — Master J Cozanet
Schooner Renard — Master D Brevrult
TS Rara Avis

Ireland
TS Asgard II — Capt C Newport

Netherlands
TS Iris — Capt B Bos
TS Europa — Master R Vos
TS Mercedes — Master O Wipperfuerth

Poland
TS Dar Mlodziezy — Master H Sniegocki
TS Pogoria — Capt A Szleminski

Russia
TS Mir — Capt V Antanov

United Kingdom
TS Bessie Ellen — Capt N Alford
TS Earl of Pembroke — Capt D Redhead
TS Kaskelot — Capt J Bates
TS Prince William — Capt L Keating
Sloop Pickle — Capt R Barton
TS Grand Turk — Capt I D MacDougal
TS Lord Nelson — Capt C Cupples
TS Royalist — Capt G Patterson
TS Tenacious — Capt S J M Catterson
TS Will — Master C Varley
TS Phoenix

United States
TS Pride of Baltimore — Capt J C Miles

NON MILITARY VESSELS

British Antarctic Survey
RRS James Clark Ross — *Capt M J S Burgan*

British Petroleum
MV British Merlin — *Capt T Johnson*

Cunard
Queen Elizabeth 2 — *Capt I McNaught*

Global Marine
CS Sovereign — *Master J Tollady*

Guernsey Sea Fisheries
MV Leopardess — *Master R Sendall*

HM Customs
HMCC Vigilant — *Cdr N Bonner*

Northern Lighthouse Board
MV Pharos — *Master E Smith*

RNLI
Severn Class Lifeboat
Trent Class Lifeboat

RMC Marine
MV Sand Harrier — *Capt P Brown*

Scottish Fishery Protection Agency
FPV Norna — *Capt J P Laycock*

Trinity House
THV Patricia — *Cdr T Dann*

Leander
MY Leander — *Capt G Cope*

Silver Sea Cruises
MV Silver Cloud — *Capt M Sangiacomo*

Miscellaneous

SS Balmoral	*Capt S Colledge*
MV Shieldhall	*Capt P Tambling*
MV Princess Caroline	
Red Jet 4	
Red Eagle	*Capt P Mercer*
ST Challenge	*Capt R Allen*
ST Brocklebank	*Capt J Temple*
Medusa	*Master M Boyce*
MTB 102	*Master R Basey*
RAF SPT 1502	*Terry Ford & Richard Hellier*
FMB 43957	*Roger Woodhams*
MV Jacinta	*Capt Barkworth*

Michael Nitz

Ships of the Royal Navy & Royal Fleet Auxiliary

Michael Nitz

The Fleet Flagship HMS Invincible was amongst the first vessels to take up position in the Solent, almost a week before the event in order to exchange salutes with each visiting warship as they arrived for the Fleet Review. Although the following days were to be very busy for the ship, her active days in the Fleet were nearing an end. The day after the review she handed over duties of Fleet Flagship to HMS Illustrious and it was announced, that following a short UK tour the ship would pay off into extended readiness in August, six months earlier than expected.

The crews of the saluting guns were kept busy as a constant armada of vessels arrived, exchanging international marks of respect for each visiting nationality - the expenditure of cartridges must have been on a scale unknown for many years!

Preparations complete, the aircraft carrier HMS Illustrious sits serenely in the anchorage the night before the big day. The ship was stationed at the centre of a vast fleet of warships from around the world, which stretched in several columns for 7 miles along the Solent. With her third mast recently added behind the second funnel, she presents quite a different silhouette to her sistership Invincible, from whom she was to assume the role of Fleet Flagship on completion of the Fleet Review.

Maritime Photographic

In recent years the Royal Navy's amphibious forces have been greatly improved and one of the busiest ships in recent years has been HMS Ocean. At 22,500 tonnes and the UK's only Amphibious Helicopter Carrier, the ship is capable of swinging from Humanitarian Relief operations right through the full spectrum of tasks to full scale warfighting. In 1998 she provided vital support for Honduras and Nicaragua after Hurricane Mitch swept through the Caribbean during Ocean's hot weather trials. She subsequently was tasked to help the victims of the Turkish earthquake before being deployed to Sierra Leone to evacuate British nationals and provide a show of force with 40 Commando, her embarked Royal Marine landing force. There followed warfighting operations in Afghanistan and Iraq which culminated in the award of the ship's sixth Battle Honour, Al Faw 2003.

Maritime Photographic

A further enhancement to the Royal Navy's amphibious capabilities has been the recent commissioning of two new Assault Ships (or Landing Platform Docks to use their proper nomenclature). Both were present at the review with Albion, seen here, providing a Force Protection command and control Headquarters. Police boats, inflatables, rigid raiders and landing craft, in addition to helicopters were regularly deployed on patrols from the vessel throughout the Review.

The Assault Ship HMS Bulwark, seen from HMS Ocean was the newest ship to be commissioned into the Royal Navy at the time of the review. After many delays at the builders she was handed over in July 2004 and became operational in May 2005. Her integral vehicle deck has the capacity to take up to six Challenger 2 tanks or around 30 armoured all-terrain tracked vehicles. A floodable well dock, has the capacity to take four utility landing craft. Four smaller landing craft are on davits, each capable of carrying 35 troops. A two-spot flight deck is able to take medium support helicopters and stow a third. The Flight Deck is capable of taking the Chinook helicopter.

Michael Nitz

Having the opportunity to see a nuclear submarine outside of its base port is quite rare, but to see three together is almost unheard of. Much of the work of the Submarine Service is shrouded in secrecy and very few people know where they go or what they get up to once they dive below the surface.

The three T class submarines at the review, HM Submarines Trafalgar (foreground), Trenchant and Turbulent are all based at Devonport.

HMS Trafalgar had just returned from the USA where she had been involved in trials of the new torpedo-tube launched Block IV Tomahawk cruise missiles. The eagle-eyed will notice that there are two large tarpaulins draped over the conning tower, doubtless concealing from public scrutiny some sensitive equipment temporarily fitted to the submarine.

Whilst the Fleet Review was a rare opportunity for the public to see a nuclear powered submarine outside of a naval base - it was also a rare opportunity for their crews to come up onto the casing while still at sea. There were four nuclear powered submarines present at the event, three RN and one French. The S class submarine HMS Sovereign was to be present - the only RN ship carrying a name of a vessel present at the Battle of Trafalgar, but a defect resulted in her having to return to port, her place being taken by HMS Trenchant, whose crew are seen here making preparations for the rehearsal - nothing being left to chance. In the background is the Type 42 destroyer HMS Exeter.

Dave Manley

As the sun sets on the eve of the Review an anonymous submarine sits quietly at anchor. In addition to Trenchant, two further T class submarines, Turbulent and Trafalgar, named in honour of the great victory in 1805, were also present. In the background can be seen the two Fort class replenishment ships RFA Fort Victoria and RFA Fort George.

Although the sun may be setting on the careers of the Type 42 destroyers, they were well represented at the Fleet Review with no less than five (Cardiff, Exeter, Southampton, Nottingham and Gloucester) being present, with a sixth (Manchester) keeping a watching brief while conducting security patrols in the Channel. One of the early Batch 1 ships is seen here to the left of the Japanese destroyer JDS Yuugiri.

Nick Newns

HMS Cardiff rides at anchor with the Romanian ship Regina Maria (ex-HMS London) to her right. This is not the first Spithead review in which a Romanian warship of this name has attended. A previous Regina Maria was present at the Coronation Review of King George VI in 1937. The Fishery Protection vessel HMS Tyne can be seen in the background.

Steve e Wright

Maritime Photographic

HMS Exeter (D89) moves out of the harbour in the days before the review to take up her position within the assembled fleet. HMS Gloucester (D96) is one of four later stretched Type 42 destroyers. The additional length in the bows is clearly evident in this shot. HMS Gloucester had a more active role in the review than many, being one of a group of vessels which steamed, in line astern, past HM the Queen.

Crown Copyright/Ministry of Defence

Dave Cullen

Once assembled the demands of the anchored warships were similar to those of a large town. Sailors needed to be moved from ship to shore, provisions had to be supplied, be it food, water, fuel or mail and even the rubbish had to be thrown out - so the binmen had to do their rounds. Even the police were on the beat - in boats! To make this happen a veritable fleet of small commercial vessels, from all around the South coast, were chartered by the Ministry of Defence. The task of moving sailors from the assembled fleet to shore was achieved using a "hub and spoke" method. Small vessels moved personnel from a set route and off loaded them onto a ferry acting as a hub, a bit like a departures and arrivals lounge, where security checks could be made and onward travel arranged.

To the left two small vessels can be seen running the "spokes" with one passing ahead of the Type 42 destroyer HMS Southampton and another alongside the Japanese detroyer JDS Yuugiri.

HMS Nottingham (top), another Type 42, awaits her turn on the round.

Crown Copyright/Ministry of Defence

By the time of the Dress Rehearsal on 27 June the sun was shining and the prospects for a glorious event the next day were looking good. The Ship's Company of the Type 23 frigate, HMS Iron Duke, cheer ship as the Royal column proceeded through the assembled ships. The timing of the event was planned to coincide with the tides around the Isle of Wight. The tidal streams are so complex that there was only a small window each day when the tidal flow allowed all of the ships to point in the same direction.

Maritime Photographic

Maritime Photographic

Two Type 23 frigates, HMS Westminster (F237) and HMS Grafton (F80) took part in an international steampast at the end of the review, a manoeuvre which just like every other aspect of the event was practiced in order to make sure that nothing would go wrong on the day. The Ship's Companies are fallen in to cheer ship wearing "half blues" (ceremonial uniform without the jacket). On the day of the review full No1 uniforms, with medals, were to be the order of the day. The thirteen remaining ships of this class form the backbone of the Royal Navy's escort force.

Crown Copyright/Ministry of Defence

Steve Wright

HMS Lancaster (F229) is seen dressed overall with her crew manning ship in anticipation of the Queen's arrival. HMS Lancaster carries an out of sequence pennant number of F229. Originally she was to carry F232, but as a Form F232 is the document used within the RN to report collisions at sea, it was felt prudent not to tempt fate!

Although she appears to be alone, HMS St Albans (right) was most certainly in the centre of things. Within 500 metres of her were warships from India, Japan, Denmark, Pakistan, Germany and Turkey in addition to the many tall ships and small craft which were constantly criss-crossing the anchorage.

Michael Nitz

HMS Montrose arrived at Spithead fresh from an action packed couple weeks. After a rendezvous with the Russian destroyer RFS Admiral Levchenko off Torbay a series of Officer of the Watch Manoeuvres were conducted prior to escorting the Russian ship to Brest where they both took part in Exercise Frukus 05. An annual four nation exercise (UK, France, US and Russia) it included several days "at sea" training combined with "international" sports events ashore. HMS Montrose's sports prowess came to the fore winning four out of the five events and taking the overall trophy.

Crown Copyright/Ministry of Defence

The three Hunt class vessels of the recently disbanded Northern Ireland Patrol Squadron found themselves employed on security duties around the Solent anchorage throughout the event. Although they were a common sight ploughing between the columns of assembled ships HM Ships Brecon (above), Dulverton (right) and Cottesmore were hard at work, and not a part of the assembled International Fleet. Four further Hunt class ships, however, HM Ships Cattistock, Chiddingfold, Ledbury and Middleton did take part.
The minesweeping force was further represented by seven of the eight Sandown class Single Role Mine Hunters (SRMH). Some such as HMS Shoreham, had an operational role to play before taking their place in the review lines, conducting Route Surveys in the Solent to ensure that the vast anchorage was safe.
HMS Ramsey, on the other hand was given the job of undertaking 'sheepdog' duties on the day of the review, making her responsible for ensuring that all the tall ships had weighed anchor on time so that they could then sail past HM The Queen, embarked in HMS Endurance
The other SRMHs present were HM Ships, Bangor, Grimsby, Pembroke and Penzance.
The sixteen strong Royal Navy Mine Countermeasures force is comprised entirely of ships with Glass Re-inforced Plastic hulls, earning them the collective soubriquet of the "Tupperware Navy."

Nick Hall

Walter Sartori

Russ Price

Russ Price

Russ Price

Although a much reduced force in the Royal Navy, a few of the remaining Mine Countermeasure Vessels were in attendance. In wartime they would be responsible for ensuring that sea lanes and access to ports, vital for our maritime trade (95% of our imports still arrive by sea), were kept clear of mines. In recent years RN MCM vessels have been at the sharp end of operations, clearing mines in the Persian Gulf throughout both Gulf Wars and closer to home, clearing away mines and ordinance left over from the Cold War in the ports and coastal waters of the Baltic States.HMS Cottesmore (M32) is a patrol ship conversion of a standard Hunt class vessel, losing her sweep gear, which was replaced by two inflatable boats and their associated handling equipment. Toghter with her two similarly converted sisters (HM Ships Brecon and Dulverton) they were used to operate on anti-terror patrols off Northern Ireland. With that conflict apparently over, the three ships were due to be paid off shortly after the review. HM Ships Cattistock (M31), Middleton (M34) and Chiddingfold (M37) retain their MCM equipment.

Russ Price

Russ Price

Compare the sweep decks of HMS Cattistock (above) and HMS Ledbury (top right) with the Patrol vessels on the previous page, whose sweep gear has been replaced by boats and their associated derricks.

Maritime Photographic

Maritime Photographic

Above left is the Single Role Minehunter of the Sandown class, HMS Ramsey, steaming past the Turkish Frigate Orucreis. To the right is the one that got away. Regrettably HMS Grimsby was the only RN vessel for which we couldn't find a photograph taken during the T200 commemorations, so for completeness have used an earlier image of the ship entering Portsmouth Harbour.

Walter Sartori

HMS Penzance

Russ Price

HMS Shoreham

Walter Sartori

HMS Walney

Russ Price

HMS Pembroke - the smoke coming from the stern is from a ship's company barbeque.

Walter Sartori

Commissioned in 1981 the Offshore Patrol Vessel HMS Leeds Castle was nearing the end of her career with the Royal Navy and was a rare sight around the UK. She had spent most of her life patrolling the waters around the Falklands Islands, a task she shared with her sistership HMS Dumbarton Castle. She returned to the UK for the last time earlier in 2005 and was due to be replaced by a new vessel, HMS Clyde, being built at Portsmouth by Vosper Thornycroft. HMS Leeds Castle conducted security patrol duties throughout the period of the Fleet Review.

Don Gilham

HMS Tyne is one of three new River class Offshore Patrol Vessels, employed primarily on Fishery Protection duties with the capacity to operate in other roles. Fishery Protection duties include undertaking patrols in English, Welsh and Northern Irish waters enforcing UK and EU fisheries legislation. Two man teams conduct boardings of fishing vessels inspecting net sizes, weight of catches, fish sizes, composure of catches and the vessel's logbook and licence. The River class were built by Vosper Thornycroft (VT) in Southampton under an innovative arrangement, whereby the ships are leased to the Royal Navy under a five-year agreement which includes VT taking responsibility for maintenance and support during the period.

Walter Sartori

A minnow amongst giants.....HMS Gleaner is the smallest vessel in commission in the Royal Navy and was most probably the smallest commissioned vessel present at the Review. This 22 ton vessel was commissioned on 5 December 1983 and is based at Devonport. She was designed to conduct inshore surveys along the south coast of England but has since spent time surveying around the entire coastline of Great Britain and has visited various ports in Europe.

David Smith

HMS Roebuck was built by Brooke Marine at Lowestoft, and entered service with the Royal Navy in July 1986. Built as a Coastal Survey Vessel primarily for surveying UK waters she has since seen extensive world-wide deployments from the Gulf to North America. The ship underwent an extensive refit and modernisation package at Devonport in early 2005, which saw her upgraded sufficiently to remain available to the Royal Navy for a further 10 years. The ship's primary role consists of directed operational tasks as a Fleet Unit in support of Amphibious Warfare (AW) operations, conducting Rapid Environmental Assessments (REA) (surveys to facilitate tactical exploitation of the environment by maritime and joint forces) and Mine Counter Measures Tasking Authority (MCMTA) support. These roles are in addition to her core output, Military Hydrographic Data gathering. In 2005 the ship was awarded the battle honour Iraq 2003 for her work in the waters off Iraq.

Maritime Photographic

At 13,500 tonnes, the Royal Navy's largest survey ship, HMS Scott, took a central role in the review forming part of the Royal Review Column of ships sailing between the lines of assembled ships. In her role as a VIP ship she embarked more than 80 Heads of Navies and their guests for the occasion - in addition to hosting the Duke and Duchess of Cornwall.

Nick Newns

The P2000 class training boats of the 1st Patrol Boat Squadron were in much demand throughout the event and could be seen dashing around the anchorage on a wide variety of tasks. More used to taking groups of University students to sea for training cruises, the boats were used as VIP transports, Media platforms and for the occasional security patrol. One of the 9 boats deployed to Portsmouth for the event was HMS Explorer seen here with her crew dressed in "full blues" running into a freshening wind. This vessel is assigned to the Yorkshire University Royal Naval Unit, hence the white rose on the after superstructure.

Steve Wright

HMS Raider. is attached to Cambridge URNU

Walter Sartori

HMS Ranger, which together with her sister HMS Trumpeter (below) used to operate from Gibraltar on security duties, is now attached to Sussex URNU.

Walter Sartori

HMS Tracker can more normally be found operating with the Oxford URNU.

Walter Sartori

HMS Trumpeter is now attached to Bristol URNU.

Walter Sartori

HMS Blazer operates with the Southampton URNU. The blue flag being flown from the port yard arm is the Trafalgar 200 flag, which was worn by all vessels at the Fleet Review.

Neill Rush

HMS Archer is attached to Aberdeen URNU. Many of these small craft perpetuate names that were carried by Escort Carriers in the Second World War.

Neill Rush

HMS Puncher is attached to the London URNU.

Don Gilham

HMS Example operates on behalf of the Northumbria URNU.

Crown Copyright/Ministry of Defence

The Aviation Training Ship, RFA Argus, seen here with the French tanker FS Meuse and the Romanian frigate Regina Maria, was one of the hubs for the processing of personnel from ship to shore. Responsible for ships in Zone D she co-ordinated the liberty boats from the Italian sail training ship Amerigo Vespucci, the Russian destroyer RFS Admiral Levchenko, FS Meuse, the Dutch LPD HrMs Rotterdam, the Pakistani ship PNS Tippu Sultan, the Greek ship HS Hydra and the sail training ships from India and Brazil, INS Tarangini and NE Cisne Branco respectively.

Nick Newns

RFA Fort George is one of two "one stop" auxiliaries operated by the Royal Fleet Auxiliary, able to supply fuel, provisions and ammunition to warships while underway. These 31,500 tonne ships are a key part of any major naval Task Group and are now frequently deployed with Merlin helicopters, acting as a force multiplier, thereby becoming an even greater operational asset.

Nick Hall

RFA Orangeleaf was representative of the tankers operated by the RFA for providing fuel at sea. These "Leaf" class tankers are commercial designs fitted with a refuelling station amidships offering the ability to refuel a vessel on each side. Their large fuel capacity also makes them ideal for ferrying fuel between bases worldwide.

Nick Newns

RFA Sir Galahad is one of only three LSLs remaining in service with the RFA in 2005. Although the class entered service in in the late 1960s the three remaining ships are a far cry from the class "originals". RFA Sir Galahad, herself is a new build ship, built in 1987 to replace the original vessel that was sunk in the 1982 Falklands War. She is unique amongst her sisters in that she has a visor type bow door which rises upwards in one piece, as opposed to the conventional opening doors of the remainder of the class.

Russ Price

RFA Sir Tristram, one of the original LSLs, was extensively damaged in 1982 in the same attack that destroyed RFA Sir Galahad. She was returned to the UK at the end of the war and extensively rebuilt to continue in service. With waterline access to the ship via her stern ramp, she was also employed as a hub ship at the review, this time serving Zone A and the assembled RN, Pakistani, Omani, Polish, French and Danish crews.

Steve Wright

RFA Wave Ruler formed part of the International Fleet Review columns after replenishing many vessels of the visiting Navies, such as the Japanese Training Squadron and the US Navy assault ship USS Saipan, before the event, in the English Channel. Special guests hosted for the day were the Mayor and Mayoress of Scarborough; the ship's affiliated town and the ship's Lady Sponsor, Mrs Geoff Hoon - with husband - who launched the ship in February 2001.

Maritime Photographic

MV Hurst Point was one of six vessels built for the MoD under an October 2000 contract for the supply of six ro-ro vessels to meet the requirements for stategic sealift capabilities. Under a 25 year private finance initiative deal, AWSR Shipping Limited were contracted to build and run the vessels for the MoD. The contract, likely to be worth up to £950 million, was finally signed on 27 June 2002. The MoD will normally use four of the ships, with all six being available for operations. All six of the ships have this green hull, white superstructure, yellow funnel colour scheme and fly the Red Ensign.

Russ Price

Mother hen looking after her brood - In addition to being the official RFA host ship for the event, the Logistic Landing Ship RFA Sir Galahad acted as a Hub vessel for Zone C ships. As can be seen here a multitude of small vessels brought crew to her for transfer to shore, using various larger craft (the yellow charter vessel to the right is one such craft, the Maid of Poole). Zone C Warships included the Japanese destroyers JDS Murasame and JDS Yuugiri, the Type 42s HMS Southampton and HMS Nottingham, the Spanish SPS Blas de Lezo and the sail training ships Shabab Oman and Iskra.

Security arrangements for the assembled fleet were on a scale never seen in the Solent before - but in the light of subsequent bombings in London just a few days later, obviously very essential to the event. The Royal Marines, MoD Police and others, provided Force Protection to over 150 vessels anchored between Portsmouth and the Isle of Wight. They are seen here showing the assembled media that they meant business!

Crown Copyright/Ministry of Defence

Don Gilham

The overall security operation comprised vessels of all shapes and sizes, most purpose built for their roles of fast interception, but many chartered or redeployed from bases further afield to provide sufficient coverage. Both the military and civilian authorities co-ordinated to place a security cordon around the anchorage in order to provide a safe and secure haven for the visiting warships. Pre event planning and exercises took place in an effort to draw up procedures for dealing with any scenario, be it terrorist threat, protestors, or just the over keen daytripper getting too close. As part of the force protection provided to the assembled fleet the Hampshire Police put on an exercise showing how they would deal with a group of protestors attempting to climb a ships anchor cable (left).

The vessel of choice for many was the Rigid Inflatable or RIB. Above can be seen one assigned to a Royal Navy Bomb Disposal team. On the opposite page can be seen, armed Royal Marine patrols, fast landing craft and a Ministry of Defence Police launch, all of which could be seen throughout the event scurrying around the anchorage.

Walter Sartori

Crown Copyright/Ministry of Defence

Don Gilham

Don Gilham

Security and Force Protection involved craft of all shapes and sizes and was an around the clock operation co-ordinated by the Hampshire Police.

Michael Nitz

As the sun began to set on 27 June all of the preparations were complete and the ships at anchor. The French aircraft carrier FS Charles de Gaulle (left), the Spanish SPS Principe de Asturias, USS Saipan and, just visible HMS Invincible sit at the head of the review, portraying the truly international flavour of the gathering.

Michael Nitz

While the rest of the fleet settle down for the evening, the Assault Ship HMS Albion remained a hive of activity with regular rotation of Force Protection personnel and their craft maintaining their constant vigil around the anchorage. SPS Principe de Asturias can be seen ahead of the ship.

Access through the fleet for the public in yachts and pleasure craft was very restricted but some of the best views were obtained by passengers on the regular Portsmouth to Isle of Wight car ferries, whose route took them through the assembled ships.
Here the Wightlink ferry St Clare can be seen passing between HMS Ocean and HMS Albion. In the distance are the French carrier FS Charles de Gaulle, the American Assault Ship USS Saipan and the aircraft carrier HMS Invincible. In the foreground is RFA Orangeleaf and the two Royal Fleet Auxiliary sisters RFA Fort George and RFA Fort Victoria.

(Opposite) - An aerial view of the Western end of the anchorage shows the extent of the fleet. At the extreme right is the large merchant tanker BP British Merlin, with the majority of the remaining vessels comprising escort size vessels from visiting navies and smaller Royal Navy ships.

Crown Copyright/Ministry of Defence

The Big Day Arrives

28th June 2005

Previous reviews had suffered at the hands of the UK's fickle weather, but on Tuesday 28 June the weather dawned fine, dry and sunny and as a consequence the crowds came out in their thousands to witness this "once in a lifetime" event. The foreshore beach and small boat anchorages were full, with everyone wanting a glimpse of the assembled armada and the Royal Party.

Crown Copyright/Ministry of Defence

The reviewing ships were led by the Trinity House Veseel THV Patricia, as it is the right of Trinity House to preceed the Sovereign when afloat in UK waters. With the Royal Yacht having been decommissioned (and now a museum ship at Leith) the Ice Patrol Vessel HMS Endurance had the honour of assuming the role for the occasion.

A Royal Marine band was positioned on the forward working deck of HMS Endurance. A special viewing platform had been constructed above the bridge from where the Reviewing Party could observe events. HMS Endurance is seen here passing ahead of the Type 23 frigate HMS Iron Duke, whose Ship's Company are greeting the Queen with the traditional three cheers..

With the White Ensign flying stiffly in the breeze a guard from the large Assault Ship HMS Albion (right) wait in relative comfort to salute Her Majesty.

At the other end of the spectrum, the ship's company of a mine counter-measures vessel stand in the bows of their ship, slightly closer to the elements, ready to cheer ship as the Monarch approached.

Her Majesty Queen Elizabeth II, flanked by the First Sea Lord Admiral Sir Alan West and HRH The Duke of Edinburgh observe proceedings from the specially constructed viewing platform sited above the bridge of HMS Endurance.

The crew of the large French nuclear-powered aricraft carrier FS Charles de Gaulle do everything with a "Gallic Flair." As HMS Endurance approached she was greeted by a chorus of the National Anthems from both France and the United Kingdom followed by a very rousing three cheers.

Maritime Photographic

Nick Newns

The Reviewing ships continued to head west along the Solent (above) passing the nuclear powered submarine HMS Trafalgar and the Latvian ship LNS Virsatis. The brand new Danish Flexible Support Ship HDMS Esbern Snare (below), the Korean Navy tanker ROKS Chung Jee and the Northern Lighthouse Board's ship Pharos lay at anchor, dressed overall on review day.

Steve Wright

As the afternoon progressed thunderstorms and torrential rain lashed the anchorage. The French aircraft carrier FS Charles de Gaulle and the tug FS Saire sit at anchor under ever darkening skies, while the nuclear powered submarine FS Perle appears to be heading back out to sea.

Nick Newns

(Opposite) In addition to THV Patricia and HMS Endurance, the reviewing ships comprised the frigate HMS Chatham (left), acting as Royal Guardship, followed by HMS Scott, with the Duke and Duchess of Cornwall onboard with other dignitaries and VIPs from visiting countries, RFA Sir Bedivere, HMS Enterprise and the Motor Yacht Leander. Bringing up the rear of the column and for the first time, in a freshening wind, under sail, the tall ship Grand Turk.

In addition to her role as Royal Guardship HMS Chatham also played host to some very high profile guests including the Lord Warden of the Cinque Ports, Lord Boyce, The Minister for the Armed Forces, Adam Ingram, The Permanent Under Secretary, Sir Kevin Tebbit, Chief of Defence Staff General Sir Michael Walker, the Chief of Defence Logistics General Sir Kevin O'Donahue, the Commander in Chief Fleet Admiral Sir Jonathan Band, Admiral of the Fleet Admiral Sir Julian Oswald and many others. HMS Enterprise (this page) had sailed from Marchwood, Southampton, to join the review, again with a large number of VIPs onboard including the head of several world navies including South Africa and Germany as well as senior British Military figures. His Royal Highness the Duke of York joined the ship by boat later in the day.

Michael Nitz

HMS Scott followed by MY Leander and Grand Turk pass a line of international warships headed by the Polish frigate ORP General Tadeus Kosciuszko and behind her, the South Korean destroyer ROKS Chungmugong Yi Sun-Shin.

Nick Newns

The Indian Navy's destroyer INS Mumbai fires a salute to the Queen and passing ships, while in the foreground the crew of the Japanese destroyer JDS Murasame salute Her Majesty.

The guard on HMS Ocean (above) "dress off" having fallen in, while the sailor (left) seems to be having trouble putting a name to the face. It is of course the record-breaking yachtswoman Dame Ellen McArthur, who was made an honourary Lieutenant Commander in the Royal Naval Reserve, fallen in with the rest of the Ship's Company aboard HMS Ocean.

There were over 1200 people on board HMS Ocean for the event, which included 270 recruits from HMS Raleigh, in Cornwall, who had only been in the Royal Navy for 8 weeks, and 50 officer cadets from Britannia Royal Naval College, Dartmouth. As well as being the IFR's media ship with over 200 of the world's press embarked, the ship also had the honour of being the Flagship for Lieutenant General Sir Robert Fulton KBE and his guests who included Lieutenant Commander Dame Ellen McArthur RNR and Sir Matthew Pinset.

"Navigator's Yeoman to the bridge - at the rush!" - It may look as though there has been a slight navigational error, but rest assured HMS Endurance had plenty of room to pass astern of the American Helicopter Carrier USS Saipan.

Although originally it was intended that HMS Scott would be nominated as a media vessel, in the end the role fell to the fleet of P2000 patrol craft. Consequently throughout the review a pair of these small craft were jostling for position to provide the media with the best possible pictures - although HMS Scott would have been a more stable platform, the photographers would not have been able to move along the column as the P2000s were able. There was only one rule - you can go where you like but don't overtake THV Patricia!

Nick Newns

The huge bulk of the Royal Fleet Auxiliary "one stop" replenishment vessel RFA Fort Victoria. The Vulcan Phalanx gun, which can be seen on the bridge roof, is mounted where the Seawolf Type 911 tracker was designed to go. The rather empty top of the foremast was to have carried a search radar as part of the same weapon system. Amidships, between the refuelling gantries, there are positions for installing vertical launch Seawolf. Unfortunately none of this equipment was ever fitted. Notice that many of her boats are swung out on their davits. The ship to the right is the Dutch assault ship HrMs Rotterdam.

Nick Newns

The Motor Yacht Leander owned by Sir Donald Gosling, a great supporter of and benefactor to, the Royal Navy, is seen passing the Japanese destroyer JDS Murasame and in close company with a P2000 training boat of the 1st Patrol Boat Squadron which are attached to University Royal Naval Units along the length and breadth of the country.

Nick Newns

The landing ship RFA Sir Bedivere was also a part of the Review Column and is seen here in company with HMS Example and rigid raiders of the Force Protection team. Unusually for a ship underway the accommodation ladder is down and it appears that a personnel transfer might have been about to take place.

Steve Wright

The African continent is represented here by the Moroccan frigate Mohammed V (611), the Algerian corvette El Kirch (353) and behind her the Nigerian frigate NNS Aradu (F89). By the time the review column had reached this point the wind was freshening and the storm clouds were gathering. The thunderstorms and torrential rain that meteorologists had predicted for the day of the review, were, it would seem, on their way.

How times have changed - The Russian destroyer RFS Admiral Levchenko with her crerw manning the sides. Perhaps this picture more than any other in this book shows the common bond shared by sailors throughout the world and why perhaps this international gathering was such a success. Old adversaries - New friends. The event was also aimed at getting youngsters closer to the action and to give them a first hand experience of naval life. Perhaps this young cadet will be the first of the new generation of sailor - ready to continue the traditions of the Royal Navy - and maintain the high regard in which the RN is held worldwide.

Nick Hall

The Canadian frigate HMCS Montreal nears the Cunard liner Queen Elizabeth 2. There had been press stories that passengers aboard were unhappy with the location of the liner as they had been promised that they would be in the centre of the action - however as she arrived on the morning of the review, the Captain elected to stay in deeper water to give his ship a bit more sea room. In the event, the Royal Party, in HMS Endurance sailed out to the QE2 to start the review.

Nick Newns

The last hurrah - There were many poignant moments but none so more than this with the crew of the Type 42 destroyer, HMS Cardiff, saluting their monarch as she passes in HMS Endurance. This was perhaps one of the last cermonial duties performed by the crew of the destroyer as she decommissioned within days of the end of the review after 26 years service with the Royal Navy.

Nick Newns

The Japanese destroyer JDS Yuugiri and the landing ship RFA Sir Galahad sit close off the foreshore at Gosport. These two ships were pretty much in the middle of the review with ships stretching at least three miles to either side of them.

Nick Newns

Maritime Photographic

The large and the small - Some of the heavier ships, the French tanker FS Meuse (A607), RFA Argus, HMS Illustrious, SAS Drakensberg and HMS Bulwark ride at anchor, while to the right the Dutch minehunter HrMs Urk sits at the end of a line of international mine counter measures vessels, from Germany, Belgium, Lithuania and Latvia.

Crown Copyright/ Ministry of Defence

Nick Newns

(This page and opposite) A novel feature of this review was the effort to make it morte dynamic. This was achieved by including a sailpast of warships through the review lines. Lead by HMS Cumberland (F85), the column included HMAS Anzac (150), HMS Gloucester (D96), HMCS Montreal (336) and HM Ships Westminster (F237) and Grafton (F80). At speeds of 17 knots some precision station keeping was required.

Nick Newns

Bringing up the rear of the review colum was the tall ship Grand Turk, representing Nelson's flagship HMS Victory for the event. Throughout the previous days and during the rehearsal the ship had to steam under her auxiliary motor, but come the day of the event, under darkening skies and freshening winds, the ship was able to rig some canvas, making a tremendous sight as she emerged from between the lines of assembled modern day warships.

Crown Copyright/ Ministry of Defence

A flypast concluded the formal review, with the assembled aircraft flying an east to west track along the Solent under a very low overcast sky.

Formations included aircraft from the Maritime Group which included an RAF E-3 Sentry and two Tornado F3s, followed by six other formations which included, a VC-10, Nimrod, Jaguars and Typhoon in addition to Jetstreams.

The fixed wing element also included a mixed formation of RAF Harrier GR7 from 3 Squadron and Royal Navy FA2 Sea Harriers from 801 NAS, as seen here in a diamond nine formation, the four aircraft forming the small aft inner diamond are Sea Harriers.

The flypast also included a rotary wing element comprising Chinook, Merlin, Sea King and Lynx. The final formation included the Australian Navy Seahawk, a Pakistani Sea King and a Danish Lynx. They were joined by a civilian owned Westland Wasp.

The highlight of the day for many was the "Son et Lumiere" which attracted huge crowds - some estimates putting the numbers in excess of 250,000. Heavy showers having passed and with the weather now dry and the cloudbase retreating upwards all was set fair for a spectacular re-enactment of the Battle of Trafalgar. To the accompaniment of music and a stirring narration by Robert Hardy the tall ships sailed along the Southsea seafront, exchanging pyrotechnic broadsides as the ships proceeded toward the harbour.......

At the climax of the battle a massive firework display was staged from barges moored offshore as laser lights sent beams of blue light into the night skies. It was a fitting and spectacular end to a day of events designed to commemorate the Battle of Trafalgar, and the life and death of its architect - Admiral Lord Nelson.

By 2230 the display was over. On the water many hundreds of small spectator craft began to make their orderly way back to their home ports and marinas - and the many thousands of spectators began to make the long trek home - and for many it was to be a very long trek. Swamped by the huge numbers attending, the transport system couldn't cope and for many it would be nearly 0300 the following morning before they finally reached their cars or boarded their trains - but little would dampen the memories of such a spectacular night.

Nick Hall

Visiting Warships

Nick Newns

Walter Sartori

The international nature of the Fleet Review attracted many ships which are very rarely, if ever, seen in the waters around the United Kingdom. Some afforded the first opportunity to see such a vessel, others were very exotic - while a few were just - well, quite unexpected!

The Algerian missile corvette El Kirch, seen on this page falls into the category of exotic. Rarely seen outside of the coastal waters of the Mediterranean, this vessel is quite an amalgamation of nationalities. Although the hull appears to be of a Spanish design, the ship was built in Algeria, with Bulgarian assistance. She is fitted with Chinese C802 Saccade missiles at the stern and mounts a Russian 76mm gun on the forecastle.

Commissioned in 2002 she is powered by diesel engines which drive the vessel through three shafts at speeds up to 31 knots.

Maritime Photographic

Getting the award for attending from the greatest distance, the Australian frigate HMAS Anzac attended the review as part of a more ranging six month deployment, Operation Northern Trident 2005. She sailed from Australia in March visiting Goa, the Red Sea, Egypt and Crete before stopping off in Turkey to take part in commemorations at Gallipoli for the Australian troops killed in that dreadful campaign. Various stops in the Mediterranean followed before participation in Exercise Neptune Warrior off the coast of Scotland. On completion of the International Fleet Review and the International Festival of the Sea at Portsmouth, the ship began the long trek home, where she arrived in August.
HMAS Anzac is one of ten Anzac class frigates built for Australia (8) and New Zealand (2), in a programme that should see the last ship HMAS Perth, delivered in 2006. The class is based on the very successful German Meko design, several variations of which were on display at the review serving with a variety of nations.

Steve Wright

Walter Sartori

Nick Newns

The small Belgian Navy were represented by three ships in the Solent. The frigate BNS Westdiep (F911) is one of two remaining in service, the third having been transferred to the Bulgarian Navy. These small frigates have given over 30 years sterling service to the Belgians and are shortly to be replaced by two former Dutch frigates, both larger and more modern than the small Weilingen class. The remaining two frigates in Belgian service are likely to join their sister in service with the Bulgarian Navy.

The mine counter measures vessel BNS Narcis (M923) is one of the Tripartite class of vessel, so called because they were built under a collaborative programme between the French, Belgian and Dutch Navies. These ships have a GRP hull similar to the Royal Navy ships. Three of the Belgian ships have been transferred to the French Navy to bolster their MCM numbers.

The third Belgian visitor was the Depot Ship, BNS Godetia (A960). Completed in 1966 she is now rated as a Command and Logistic Support Ship, able to parent a squadron of MCMV's or to act independently - in recent years she has conducted humanitarian deployments to West Africa. She is no stranger to these shores, or indeed to fleet reviews, having been present at the last Spithead review, the Silver Jubilee Review of 1977.

Maritime Photographic

Although there were many tall ships at the review, only a handful were operated by the military as training ships. One such vessel is NE Cisne Branco which is operated by the Brazilian Navy. Despite her appearance she is a newly built vessel, being completed in 2000 by Damen Shipyards in Holland. She has auxiliary diesel power, but can rig up to 2,195 square metres of canvas when under full sail. There seemed to be some serious "oneupmanship" amongst the tall ships contingent with regard to ensign size - despite appearances, the Brazilian Navy didn't quite get the title in the "Biggest Ensign Flown" competition!

Maritime Photographic

The Canadian Navy are regular visitors to these shores and as standing member of NATO's Standing Naval Force Atlantic frequently operate with Royal Navy ships. HMCS Montreal is one of 12 Halifax class frigates in service with the navy and form the backbone of their surface escort fleet. Completed in 1994 she is armed with 8 Harpoon anti-ship missiles, 4 of which can be seen abaft the funnel; 8 launchers for the Sea Sparrow anti-air missile, in addition to a 3-inch gun and torpedo tubes. The ship can operate a helicopter up to Sea King size from its flight deck.

(Opposite) Another South American navy to operate a Sail Training Ship is Colombia, who attended with ARC Gloria, a barque rigged ship built in Bilbao in 1969. This 1.250 ton, all welded hull vessel has a sail area of 1,675 square metres. Similar vessels are in service with Ecuador, Mexico and Venezuela. With regards to the "Biggest Ensign Flown" competition, I think we might have a winner here!

Maritime Photographic

Steve Wright

Seen for the first time in the UK was the Royal Danish Navy's new Flexible Support Ship HDMS Esbern Snare. Commissioned only a month before the review, this large ship is quite a departure for the Danish Navy who have not previously operated a vessel of this size. The innovative design sees a vessel with armament equivalent to a frigate, a flight deck and hangar sufficient to operate two Merlin helicopters (see the picture above how the Lynx appears lost on the flight deck) and internal space to accomodate vehicles and troops together with the Ro-Ro facilities to embark and disembark them. Add to this the command and control facilities, ability to lay mines, or to operate as a hospital ship, this ship, together with her sister HDMS Absalon, confer a true multi-mission flexibility upon the Danish Navy.

Steve Wright

Having regained independence in 1991, the fledgling Estonian Navy was represented by ENS Admiral Pitka (A230), the Flagship of their fleet. A former Danish Naval vessel (HDMS Beskyterren) she was transferred as a gift in 2000, being commissioned into the Estonian Navy in November of that year. The ship is operated primarily as a command and support vessel overseeing the operations of this mainly coastal naval force.

The minelayer Pohjanmaa (01) belongs to the very colourful Finnish Navy. They are rare amongst modern navies in so far as the majority of their combat vessels wear a predominatly green camouflage scheme. Though in the days of radar this might seem a little superflous, much of this navies operations are conducted in coastal waters and inland waterways, where the green blends very well with the forested coastline. Completed in 1979 Pohjanmaa also operates as a training ship, in which role she can carry an additional 70 cadets in temporary accommodation fitted on the minedecks.

Maritime Photographic

As would be expected at such a commemoration, the largest contingent from overseas came from the French Navy who sent five warships, in addition to several sail training vessels, to the event. The largest of these, and the largest warship in a European Navy, was the nuclear-powered aircraft carrier FS Charles de Gaulle. At around 42,000 tonnes full load this impressive ship can carry Super Etendard and Rafale jet fighters in addition to Hawkeye AEW aircraft and the full range of French naval helicopters. With her decks manned and the Tricolour proudly flying in the breeze the vessel dominated the eastern end of the review lines. The ship had recently returned from exercises off the eastern seaboard of the USA throughout which she was escorted by the Type 42 destroyer HMS Nottingham.

Another French visitor was the Air Defence destroyer FS Jean Bart. Completed in 1991. Both ships of this class are basically a re-run of the Georges Leygues Anti-submarine frigates, but modified to carry a larger air search radar, mounted above the funnel, which now exhausts to each side, and long range anti-air missiles. These ships form an integral part of any French Carrier Task Group and are scheduled to be replaced by newly constructed Horizon class destroyers from about 2012.

Nick Newns

The Underway Replenishment tanker FS Meuse is one of the successful French designed Durance class, examples of which are now in service witrh Argentina, Australia and Saudi Arabia. At 17,900 tons full load, these tankers can perform a variety of replenishment tasks, including fuel, water, provisions and ammunition. They are also able to operate a small helicopter.

Michael Nitz

Steve Bush

The only other European country to operate nuclear powered submarines, the French Navy sent FS Perle (top) to the review, one of 6 Rubis class attack submarines. These relatively small submarines can carry torpedoes and Exocet missiles and can reportedly dive to depths in excess of 300 metres.
The smallest French participant was the coastal tug FS Saire (A676) One of up to 22 vessels of this class she was on hand to provide support to the nuclear-powered submarine.

Maritime Photographic

The modernisation of the German Navy continues apace and FGS Sachsen is one of the new generation Type 124 Air Defence ships built to replace the American designed Lutjens class. Commissioned in November 2004 FGS Sachsen was the first of the three ship class. Her pyramid shaped masts carry a 3-D air search radar (after mast) and a phased array surface search radar on the foremast. The shape of the masts exemplify the stealth characteristics of these ships.

Don Gilham

Unlike most of the mine warfare vessels seen in this book so far, the German Navy Type 332 class coastal minehunters, as exemplified here by FGS Frankenthal, are not built of GRP. The 12 ships of the class, together with the 5 vessels of the Type 333 and 5 vessels of the Type 352 classes, are constructed of amagnetic steel as used in the submarine building industry. FGS Frankenthal was commissioned in December 1992, replacing older wooden hulled minesweepers, a material that had become the norm during the Second World War.

Maritime Photographic

The ever expanding Royal Hellenic Navy was represented by the Meko 200HN class frigate HS Hydra. Very similar to HMAS Anzac the four Greek ships were delivered between 1992 and 1998, HS Hydra having been builtin Germany and the remainder in Greece. In recent years Greek warships have become regular visitors to the UK undertaking much of their sea training under the auspices of the Royal Navy's Flag Officer Sea Training organisation operating from Devonport in the south west of the country.

Nick Hall

Another rapidly expanding navy, though this time on the Asian continent is that of the Indian Navy. For many years a customer of the former Soviet Union, the Indian Navy is now beginning to produce their own ships, including an aircraft carrier, whose keel was recently laid down in India. INS Mumbai (D62) is the latest of three Delhi class destroyers, designed and built in India and incorporating weapons and electronics from both east and west. Completed in 2001 these large destroyers are very heavily armed and capable vessels, able to launch up to 16 surface-to-surface missiles and to carry and operate two Sea King sized helicopters. In recent years the Indian Navy have begun to change from their tradition dark grey hull to a more pleasing light grey scheme.

Maritime Photographic

Walter Sartori

Two more naval operated sail training ships were the INS Tarangini (India) and the KRI Dewa Ruci (Indonesia). INS Tarangini (above) was built in India in 1997 based on a three masted barque. She frequently undertakes distant training cruises from her Mumbai base. By comparison KRI Dewa Ruci is a steel hulled Barquentine which was built in Hamburg in 1953.

Russ Price

The Irish Naval Service was represented by the Offshore Patrol Vessel LE Eithne (pronounced Etna). A small force of mainly coastal vessels, the Irish Naval Service provide security patrols and fishery protection duties around Irelands' extensive coastline. Built in 1984 LE Eithne was the last vessel to be completed by Verolme of Cork.

Nick Hall

Russ Price

Maritime Photographic

Two very different vessels were present from the Italian Navy. The submarine ITS Giuliano Prini was the only conventionally powered submarine present. Built in 1989 to an Improved Sauro design the submarines of this class are able to launch torpedoes and the ability to launch Harpoon or Exocet missiles could be refitted on the later submarines of the class. The sail training ship ITS Amerigo Vespucci is a real veteran, having been completed in 1931. Of all steel construction she regularly embarks on training cruises with up to 150 trainees embarked. She has also attended a previous fleet review at Spithead, this time the 1953 Coronation Fleet Review.

Nick Newns

One of the highlights of the review was the arrival of a Japanese Training Squadron. Under the command of Rear Admiral Masahiro Shibara the three ship squadron, comprising the destroyers JDS Murasame (above) and JDS Yuugiri (right) together with the training ship JDS Kashima included 750 men, 180 of whom were recently promoted Junior Officers. The ships had left Tokyo in April for a five month round the world training cruise, stopping at ports in the Pacific, Atlantic, Mediterranean and the Indian Ocean before returning to Tokyo in September.

Michael Nitz

JDS Yuugiri was completed in 1989 as one of the eight-ship Asagiri class, although two (Asagiri and Yamagiri) have subsequently been converted to training ships. For her size JDS Yuugiri is very well armed, carrying Harpoon, ASROC, Sea Sparrow, torpedoes and an Oto-melara gun, with a flightdeck and hangar able to accommodate a Seahawk helicopter; all on a hull of 3,500 tons.

Nick Newns

The 4,000 ton training ship JDS Kashima was commissioned in 1995, during which year she conducted her inaugural world tour. Powered by Rolls-Royce Spey gas turbines and 2 Mitsubishi diesels she can cruise at 18 kts for 7,000 miles. She has accommodation for 140 Midshipmen.

Maritime Photographic

Maritime Photographic

A Navy rarely seen operating around the UK is that of South Korea. The KDX-2 class destroyer ROKS Chungmoogong Yi Sun-Shin was commissioned in November 2003 appears to be a mixture of American and French infuences. Gas turbine powered and heavily armed with American missile systems and European electronics, she operates a Westland Lynx helicopter. The tanker ROKS Chun Jee was completed in 1990 and provides for underway replenishment from stations to port and starboard and can conduct replenishment of solid provisions from a flight deck, although there is no hangar to support a helicopter.

Steve Wright

Walter Sartori

Nick Newns

Another fledgling Baltic Navy is that of Latvia who have a combined Navy and Coastguard. LNS Virsaitis (A53) is the former Norwegian Minelayer KNM Vale which was transferred in 2003. Built in 1978 the ship has been modified to act as a support ship to the small mine counter measures force operated by the Latvian Navy.

Lithuania is another Baltic state putting former NATO equipment to good use. LNS Kuris (M51) (ex- FGS Marburg) is one of two former German Lindau class Minehunters now in service. The wooden hulled ship was transferred in 2000.

The frigate Mohammed V was representing the North African country of Morocco. This French Floreal class frigate was commissioned in 2002, though unlike its French counterparts mounts a 76mm gun in place of the 100mm mounted on the French ships. The ship's AS 565MA Panther helicopter can be seen ranged on the flightdeck.

Steve Bush

Perhaps the biggest, but most welcome, surprise was the arrival in the anchorage of the Nigerian frigate NNS Aradu. Although her intention to participate was announced a long time ahead of the event, many in naval circles doubted that the ship would arrive. A Meko 360 built in Germany, the ship was commissioned in 1982 but has had a very patchy career ever since. In 1987 she suffered two groundings and a collision. Following a lengthy refit she again ran aground in 1994 and by 1995 was assessed as being beyond economic repair. She had rarely ventured to sea in the intervening periods and there had been reports that she was being used for some less than solubrious activites in the interim. In recent years efforts had been made to restore the ship to a seaworthy state, and her arrival in the Solent late on 26 June was evidence of the tremendous effort put into getting the vessel back to sea - although the vessel was looking “tired” (note the canvas hangar door) the crew were evidently proud of their ship and of their participation at the review. The ship began its delayed return to Nigeria in early July - with a portable diesel generator strapped to the middle of the flightdeck!

Walter Sartori

Maritime Photographic

Walter Sartori

One of the larger European warships on display was the Dutch amphibious ship HrMs Rotterdam (L800). Built in Holland and commissioned in 1998 she was designed to transport a fully equipped Marine battalion with docking facilities for landing craft and a flightdeck capable of handling two helicopters, whilst the hangar can accommodate up to six. The design of this vessel was the basis for the four new Bay class vessels under construction in the UK to replace the elderly 'Sir' class landing ships for the Royal Fleet Auxiliary in 2006/07.

Another Dutch participant was the Tripartite class mine counter measures vessel HrMs Urk (M861), one of fifteen vessels from the three nation programme built for the Netherlands, although only ten remain in service. HrMs Urk was commissioned in 1986.

The sail training ship Shabab Oman (right) was built in 1971 in Scotland as Captain Scott and used by a charity for sail training. Commissioned into the Omani Navy in 1979 this topsail schooner regularly embarks on training voyages with up to 24 trainees.

Russ Price

Maritime Photographic

Nick Hall

A good example of a heavily armed coastal corvette, as used by many of the smaller Gulf States, is RONV Al Mua'zzar (Q32 opposite top) which was built by Vosper Thornycroft at Woolston in the late 1990s for Oman. Of only 1,450 tons the ship is capable of speeds up to 28 knots and is armed with eight Exocet surface-to-surface missiles, an eight cell Crotale surface-to-air missile launcher, a 3-inch gun, two 20mm guns and six torpedo tubes.

The Pakistan Navy arrived with two ships, and although the Pakistanis rarely operate around the UK, the two ships are no strangers to these parts. The tanker PNS Moawin (20) is the former Dutch fast tanker HrMS Poolster, acquired by Pakistan in 1994. The second ship was the Type 21 frigate PNS Tippu Sultan (185), the former Royal Navy frigate HMS Avenger. Transferred to Pakistan in 1994, together with the remaining five of the class she has not been back to UK shores in the intervening years.She has been modified somewhat since her RN service by the addition of the Chinese LY 60N missile system forward of the bridge together with its associated radar and directors. The Seacat missile system, which was mounted on the hangar roof has been replaced by two 30mm gun mountings.

Crown Copyright/Ministry of Defence

Russ Price

A long time Soviet satellite state, Poland is gradually re-equipping with western equipment to bring her closer to NATO standards. The former USN frigate USS Wadsworth is one of two now serving with the Polish Navy. Recommissioned in 2002 ORP General Tadeusz Kosciuszko (273) is now based at Gdynia.

The Portuguese frigate NRP Alvares Cabral (F331), commissioned in 1991, is another Meko 200 frigate from the German shipbuilders of Blohm and Voss and is one of three in service with that navy.

The Portuguese sail training ship NRP Sagres (right) is another product of the German Blohm and Voss yard, but from an earlier generation. Built in 1938 as the German Albert Leo Schlageter. One of three sisters taken by the USA as reparation at the end of the Second World War, one became the USCG Eagle, another the Soviet ship Tovarisch, and the third was sold to Brazil. That vessel was brought by Portugal in 1962 and renamed Sagres. She has a sail area of over 20,000 square feet.

Maritime Photographic

Nick Newns

Another former Eastern Bloc state which is modernising with Western equipment is Romania. In 2003 they agreed to acquire two former Royal Navy Type 22 frigates in a programme that included a complete overhaul and improved combat systems. The package also included a full training programme. The first ship RS Regele Ferdinand (ex- Coventry) arrived in Romania in 2004. The second RS Regina Maria (ex-London) (above) had, by the time of the review, just completed her initial package of sea training prior to embarking on more complex training for the late summer. The ship has been fitted with a 76mm gun forward and is due to receive her remaining weapon systems during phased refits in Romania.

Nick Newns

The sinister, dark grey outlines of Russian warships are without doubt the most warlike of all present generation warships. Bristling with weapons systems and sensors these ships are the embodiment of what a warship should look like. The Udaloy class anti-submarine ship RFS Admiral Levchenko was, when in Soviet service, RFS Kharbarovsk. Based in the Northern Fleet, this vessel had recently completed a series of multi-national exercises off the French coast. After many years of under funding following the collapse of the Soviet Union, it is refreshing to see the remnants of the Russian Navy beginning to stretch their legs again with more exercises and out of area deployments planned in the future.

Walter Sartori

Steve Wright

The sail training ship Jadran (left) is another with a chequered history. Built in Germany in 1930, she was used by the Italian Navy throughout the Second World War. Having fallen into disrepair she was eventually returned to Yugoslavia where she was restored to her original configuration. Since the break up of the former Yugoslavia she is now operated by the Navy of Serbia and Montenegro.

The smallest aircraft carrier at the review was the Spanish SPS Principe de Asturias (above). Commissioned in 1988 this 17,000 ton ship can embark a combination of 6-12 Harrier aircraft or 6-10 Sea King sized helicopters. Powered by gas turbines the ship has a top speed of 25 knots.

Michael Nitz

Another newcomer to the review was the Spanish frigate SPS Blas de Lezo. The third of four Alvaro de Bazan class ships she was only commissioned in December 2004. Designed with many stealth characteristics these ships are optimised for air defence, their weapons system being centred around the American Aegis SPY-1D phased array radar system, the flat arrays of which can be seen around the superstructure at the foot of the tripod mast.

Maritime Photographic

Steve Wright

The Turkish Navy was another to arrive at the review with an example of the Meko 200 design. TCG Orucreis (F245) is seen here passing the Type 42 destroyer HMS Southampton.

The South African Navy was represented by the Fleet Replenishment Ship SAS Drakensberg (A301). She had sailed from Simon's Town on 6 June and made passage directly to the UK. En route home she visited the African ports of Lagos (Nigeria) and Luanda (Angola) for diplomatic visits. She returned to her homeport on 20 July.

Walter Sartori

Maritime Photographic

The Uruguayan sail training ship ROU Capitan Miranda (above) started life in 1930 as a clipper bowed survey vessel, before undergoing a conversion in the 1970s for service as a three masted schooner to train cadets. She is unusual in that she has superstructure for almost two thirds the length of her upperdeck.

The USCG Eagle (right) was the former Horst Wessel built by Blohm and Voss in 1938 for the German Navy. She has served with the US Coastguard since 1946 and is based at New London, Connecticut. She undertakes regular training cruises with both cadets and officer candidates embarked.

Maritime Photographic

It had been hoped that one of the USN super carriers would be at the review - in fact USS Carl Vinson had been pencilled in until the last minute, where an extension to her Gulf deployment meant that she was unable to attend. The Amphibious Assault Ship USS Saipan, which had been operating off the Scottish coast was brought in as a replacement and was the only USN representative present. Of 39,987 tons she was slightly smaller than the French carrier, though with her slab sides and high freeboard, she certainly looked bigger. USS Saipan was commissioned in1977 and has accommodation for 1700 troops and can move them ashore , together with their 45 assault vehicles, in a combination of landing craft, hovercraft and helicopters - in fact if required the assault vehicles can swim ashore as they are fully amphibious. Once ashore the ship can provide air cover with her embarked Harrier squadron.

Nick Newns

Nick Newns

Nick Newns

Several of the assembled warships brought along their embarked flights, which provided the photographer with yet more exotic military hardware. The Japanese destroyer JDS Yuugiri had a colourful SH-60J Seahawk embarked (top), while the Russian RFS Admiral Levchenko brought along a Ka-27 Helix (left). The Australian frigate HMAS Anzac was represented in the flypast by its embarked S-70B Seahawk which operated from RAF Odiham for the event.

Russ Price

Tall Ships, Merchantmen and Historic Vessels

Walter Sartori

Dave Manley

In addition to the many warships, the review lines were given that Nelsonian feel by the many Tall Ships that swelled the ranks. Over twenty -five tall ships from Sail Training Organisations, charities, charter companies to privately owned vessels joined the already mentioned military sail trainers to create a unique combination of modern military might mixed with the grace of the assembled tall ships.

The Irish Asgard II (left), a brigantine, was designed by Jack Tyrell specifically for sail training and built at Arlow, County Wicklow in 1981. Asgard II's figurehead is a carving of Granuaille, the famous 16th century Mayo sea captain and pirate queen of the sea.

The Europa (above) was built in 1911 and started life as a light ship. In 1994 she was fully re-built as a barque and now roams the oceans of the world in the best seafaring tradition. This beautiful ship has a traditional mahogany deckhouse, teakwood decks as well as the beautiful interior with authentic early 20th century details providing the perfect ambiance for a fantastic voyage. All cabins are provided with en-suite shower and toilet and there is also a hospital, deck lounge with bar, mess room and a library. The Europa's voyages regularly take her as far afield as the Antarctic, Argentina and South Africa then back again to Europe and the UK. These amazing voyages are available to individual customers looking for a fantastic ocean adventure. From time to time the Europa is also available for corporate charters and day sails.

Nick Hall

The Polish vessel, Dar Mlodziezy, has been owned by the Gdynia Maritime Academy since she was built in 1982, replacing the frigate Dar Pormoza which had trained future officers of the merchant and fishing fleets for over fifty years. Dar Mlodziezy has taken part in the Cutty Sark Tall Ships' Races many times; Her debut was in 1982 when she crossed the start line directly after being commissioned. Shortly after, she began a circumnavigation of the globe which coincided with the 200th anniversary of Australia.

Maritime Photographic

The Russian tall ship Mir, which means Peace, was built as the third of five sister ships at the Lenin-shipyard in Gdansk, Poland, based on a new type of design for square rigged training vessels. The first ship of this design was Dar Mlodziezy (see previous page). Russia then decided that she wanted a similar design for five ships as part of a trading deal with Poland. First came Druzhba and then in 1987 Mir for which the rigging design was slightly altered so that she could sail closer to the wind - up to 30 degrees rather than the usual 60 degrees for square riggers. Her full complement of sails is 26. She has sailed with a crew of 200 but can be sailed with as few as 30.

Crown Copyright/Ministry of Defence

One of the aims of this fleet gathering was to involve the youth of today. The Sea Cadet Corps' own flagship TS Royalist was one of a flotilla of tall ships adding an authentic touch of Nelson's Navy to the Trafalgar 200 curtain-raiser on the Solent. Harking back two centuries, TS Royalist joined tall ships from many nations for the evening Son et Lumiere, combining an impressive historical fleet war game complete with dramatic pyrotechnics, which really lit up the sky and gave TS Royalist an opportunity to show her paces – under broadsides of "cannon" fire.

Sea Cadets played a prominent role throughout the Royal Navy's showcase programme which also included a ceremonial Drumhead Ceremony and the International Festival of the Sea, transforming Portsmouth's historic dockyard into a maritime pageant to launch the Trafalgar 200 season of events through to the end of the year to commemorate the battle of Trafalgar and the death of Admiral Lord Nelson.

Two thousand sea cadets from over one hundred units, spread across the UK were involved in the week long spectacular; at sea aboard RN warships, assisting veterans, performing ceremonial duties and entertaining crowds of visitors back on dry land with traditional Nelson's navy customs – hornpipe dancing, club and cutlass swinging, field gun runs, window ladder display and marching bands.

Appreciation for the Sea Cadets came from many, but in particular from the First Sea Lord Admiral Sir Alan West, who commented: "I was thrilled to see such strong support from the Sea Cadets at all our Trafalgar 200 events. Their enthusiasm is infectious and I trust they enjoy supporting the Royal Navy as much as we enjoy meeting them. Their qualities of self-respect, discipline and teamwork are exactly those that Nelson embraced. We are proud to see them involved as the junior image of the Senior Service."

Dave Manley

Maritime Photographic

Don Gilham

The American topsail schooner Pride of Baltimore (top left) was built along the lines of the 1812 era Baltimore Clippers. She is used to promote tourism and economic development for Maryland and Baltimore, internationally.

The Kaskelot (above) is a replica 19th century 3 masted Barque, one of the largest remaining wooden ships in commission. Built in 1948 for the Royal Greenland Trading Company supplying the remote East Greenland coastal settlements. Subsequently she was employed as a fisheries support vessel in The Faroes. The Square Sail company purchased the vessel in 1981 and totally redesigned and re-rigged her. She is one of a small fleet of tall ships based at Charlestown in Cornwall.

Another vessel in the Square Sail fleet is the Brigantine Phoenix (left) Built by Hjorne & Jakobsen at Frederikshavn, Denmark in 1929 as an Evangelical Mission Schooner, 20 years later she retired from missionary work and carried cargo until her engine room was damaged by fire. She was bought by new owners in 1974 who converted her into a Brigantine before being purchased by Square Sail in 1988. A first aid over-haul enabled her to sail back to the UK where she underwent a complete refit.

Walter Sartori

At the end of the Battle of Trafalgar, HMS Pickle, one of the fastest vessels in the Royal Navy, raced back to England with news of the victory and the death of Admiral Lord Nelson. Making the journey from Cadiz to Falmouth in nine days, the ship's captain then hired a carriage which took him to London from the west of England in just 37 hours. Normally the journey would have taken a week. Built in 1996 in Russia, the replica, HMS Pickle (above) is a topsail schooner employed as a sail training vessel and partly continued that role with her Sea Britain 2005 tour of the UK.

The Grand Turk (right) is a replica 18th Century man-of-war of the type that took part in the Battle of Trafalgar. Built in 1996, her primary role is in the film and television industry where she has featured in such programmes as Hornblower and Longitude. In addition to film work, the Grand Turk makes a stunning venue for entertaining. Her spacious saloon is a great place for entertaining and can seat up to 120 people for dinner. On deck her traditional rigging and numerous cannons provide the backdrop for receptions for up to 200 people at the quayside.

Walter Sartori

Walter Sartori

In addition to the warships and tall ships there were also many merchantmen and historic vessels to be seen in the anchorage. The passenger vessel Balmoral was back in familiar waters. Built in Southampton in 1949 and operated under the Southampton Red Funnel Fleet for 20 years. She then moved round to the Bristol Channel where she became the last member of P&A Campbell's famous White Funnel Fleet. When they ceased operations in 1980, the ship moved to Dundee to become a floating restaurant but gradually fell into disrepair, until she was rescued by the friends & supporters of the paddle steamer Waverley. She returned to service in 1986 and now operates her main summer season in the Bristol Channel, offering day excursions to popular Coastal Resorts, as well as making visits to other ports & piers throughout the UK in Spring & Autumn.

Russ Price

Guernsey Sea Fisheries

Russ Price

Walter Sartori

Various government agencies were represented at the review. The British Antarctic Survey sent their ship RRS James Clark Ross ((top left). Fishery Protection was represented by the Leopardess (top right) of the States of Guernsey Sea Fisheries, while the Scottish Fisheries Protection Agency sent their vessel Norna (bottom left). Her Majesties Customs and Excise were represented by the new customs cutter HMCC Vigilant (bottom right).

Chris Hockaday

THV Patricia is the flagship of the Trinity House fleet. Her normal duties involve maintenance of navigational buoys, attendance and refuelling of offshore lighthouses and dealing with emergencies, including wrecks. She is fitted with special towing winches, sufficient to pull a fairly large ship away from a dangerous situation as well as providing a routine capability for moving light ships to and from their stations. She has a 20 tonne crane capable of lifting the largest navigational buoys. There is also a flightdeck aft.
She is usually based at Harwich on the East Coast but can regularly be seen at other ports around the UK. Although a working ship, this 2,500 ton vessel can carry individual fare paying passengers or corporate groups. As flagship of the Trinity House fleet Patricia is the only vessel allowed to prodceed the Royal Yacht when the monarch is embarked.

Nick Newns

The Motor Yacht Leander is owned by Captain Sir Donald Gosling KCVO Kt RNR, President of the White Ensign Association. Sir Donald, who was co-founder of National Car Parks, took delivery of vessel from Peene Werft, Germany in 1992. At 1,930 tons she was larger than many of the assembled warships. She has a steel hull and aluminium superstructure. At 75 metres long with a helicopter deck certified for 5 tonnes, she has a cruising range of 8000nm at 14.5 knots and a maximum speed of 18.5 knots. MY Leander is available for charter (reputably at in excess of £40,000 a day) in the Mediterranean or Caribbean. She has two master suites, three double guest suites, five twin guest cabins with bathrooms, a pool, a gym and a range of tenders, boats, wet bikes and jetskis. She has a crew of 24.

Nick Hall

The cable ship CS Sovereign is a multi-role vessel capable of undertaking both subsea cable maintenance and installation projects. Her open deck enables her to deploy a variety of remotely operated vehicles such as the Atlas 1 ROV. Atlas is a powerful, state of the art cable working ROV, designed for both cable maintenance and post lay and inspection roles. With 300kW of installed power they have substantial cable intervention and burial capability and a range down to 2,000m water depth. The ship is normally based at Portland, on the south coast, and provides repair and maintenance services to submarine cable systems in the Atlantic Ocean. She has a storage capacity of some 2800 cubic metres and a load capacity of 6,200 tonnes.

Nick Hall

Built in 2003 by Samsung Heavy Industries, South Korea the 250m long British Merlin is an Aframax tanker owned by BP Shipping. With a capacity of 115,000 tonnes of crude oil or fuel oil she is one of the largest merchant vessels at the review. Aframax tankers are usually between 80,000 and 120,000 deadweight tons, designed to serve different trade routes and generally engage in both medium and short-haul trades carrying crude oil. The shallower draft and shorter length of these tankers enable them to enter a greater number of ports than the larger tankers at sea today.

Russ Price

Walter Sartori

Russ Price

The Jacinta (top left) is a preserved 599 ton wet-fish stern-trawler. She was built in 1972 and is a great example of the fishing vessels that could often been seen operating from the distant water fishing ports around the UK. Throughout her career she sailed from Fleetwood, Lancashire and latterly from Hull, East Yorkshire.

The Jacinta has now been restored and put back in a sea going condition, albeit no longer in a fishing role, operating primarily as a museum ship and is normally open for visitors at her home port of Fleetwood, in the UK. She is in a fully working condition and often visits other ports around Britain and is available for private charter.

Amazon Hope 2 (above) is the second of two mercy ships converted for operating on the Amazon in South America. After the review she started on a whistlestop tour around the UK before departing for the Amazon in 2006. This former Royal Navy Fleet Diving Tender (ex-Ixworth) had recently undergone a major refit and conversion to a floating medical centre with operating theatre,dental surgery and pharmacy. The ship has been recommisioned by the Princess Royal. The original Amazon Hope (ex-Milford) has been helping to provide a healthcare system for up to 100,000 people in remote communities in Peruvian Amazon since arriving in 2001.

Operated by the Northern Lighthouse Board the 1,986 ton MV Pharos (left) was built in 1993 as a multi-purpose lighthouse tender. The ship has a helicopter deck with fire protection and fixed refuelling facilities, two cargo-holds and a main crane capable of lifting any of the buoys around the coasts of Britain.

A veteran in every sense of the word - IFR 2005 was the fourth Review that MTB102 had taken part in, the first being as escort to the Royal Barge at the Royal Review of the Reserve Fleet in 1939. At IFR 2005 MTB102 was requested by CinC Fleet to follow the frigates on the fast sailpast, a task she carried out perfectly at 20 knots 50 yards from the stern of HMS Grafton. An interesting experience! Owned and operated by the MTB102 Trust, this was no doubt the highlight of 2005 and added another chapter to the very distinguished history of this vessel. For further information see www.mtb102.com

Crown Copyright/Ministry of Defence

Russ Price

The two cruise liners Queen Elizabeth 2 and Silver Cloud, arrived in the Solent on the morning of the review to afford their passengers a grandstand seat of proceedings. At almost 80,000 tons the veteran Cunard liner QE2 was one of the largest vessels at the review.

Perpetuating the name - one of the tugs operating in the anchorage was MT Trafalgar. I have seen pictures of her in the vicinity of the French carrier FS Charles de Gaulle but have been unable to confirm whether she was one of her assigned tugs - surely the opportunity was too great to resist!

Crown Copyright/Ministry of Defence

After the Review, the assembled ship's companies eagerly awaited a message from Her Majesty, The Queen, who, as Lord High Admiral, is able to order the issue of a celebratory tot of rum to all those involved. Would those much loved and traditional three words appear in the message to the fleet? On completion of the review The Queen sent the following message of thanks to the crews of all the ships which had participated:

"It gave me great pleasure to review the international fleet assembled today at Spithead to commemorate the 200th Anniversary of the death of Admiral Lord Nelson and to witness the maritime flypast.
I was most impressed by the array of vessels and aircraft from the United Kingdom, the Commonwealth and the many nations which took part. This review reflects the true spirit of cooperation which exists between maritime nations and is a fitting symbol of the enduring legacy of the spirit of Nelson.
To those of you who have participated in this memorable event, and to all who continue to contribute to and support the many demanding operations around the world, The Duke of Edinburgh and I send our best wishes and thanks."

"Splice the Mainbrace!"

Acknowledgements

A publication such as this would have been impossible without the support of a myriad of photographers, both amateur and professional, who so willingly submitted their photographs for consideration.

Dave Cullen, Edinburgh; Gary Davies (www.maritimephotographic.co.uk), Lee-on-Solent; Fleet Photographic Unit, Royal Navy, Portsmouth; Dave Gilham, Hook; Nick Hall, Burgess Hill; Nick Newns, Plymouth; Michael Nitz, Germany; Russ Price http://russ-price.fotopic.net), Peterborough; Neill Rush, Gibraltar; Walter Sartori, Portsmouth; Steve Wright, Isle of Wight.

I must also thank the many organisations, companies, PR Officers and Ship's Companies, too numerous to mention individually, but all of whom so generously provided information for the captions. We hope you like the end result.